What are fangs?

Fangs are teeth that animals use to inject venom (poison) or to chew food. Many kinds of animals have fangs. Reptiles, mammals, and bugs are three types of animals that have them. Some animals, like snakes and spiders, use fangs for protection. Others, like dogs and pandas, use them to chew food.

In this book, you will learn about some animals with fangs. You will find out where they live, what they eat, and how big they grow.

Welcome to the wild world of fangs!

1

Reptiles are cold-blooded animals.

That means their bodies need things around them to keep them warm or cool.

Reptiles are found all over the world. There are nearly 8,000 different kinds of reptiles that walk, crawl, slither, or swim.

American Alligator

Saltwater
Crocodile

Nile Monitor

Black Mamba

REPTILES

Gaboon Viper

Cottonmouth

There are four different kinds (or orders) of reptiles:

Crocodilia (alligators and crocodiles)

Squamatas (lizards and snakes)

Testudines (turtles)

Rhynchocephalia (tuataras that live in New Zealand)

Some reptiles, like crocodiles, have teeth that look like fangs. They catch food with these big, sharp teeth.

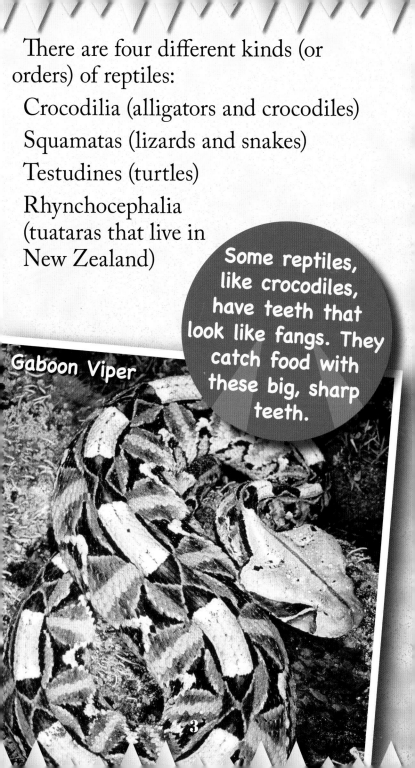

Gaboon Viper

3

Snakes—
Check It Out!

Snake fangs are hollow. They work like the needles doctors use when you get a shot. The snake bites its prey. The venom is injected into the prey through the fangs. Some fangs can be replaced as often as the snake needs them.

➤ Snakes do not have legs. Scales on their bellies help them to move.

➤ Snakes can't hear.

➤ A snake smells with its tongue.

Numbers: 2,700 different kinds

Where found: all over the world, except at the North and South Poles

Sea Snake

Green Mambas

5

Copperhead
(Agkistrodon contortrix)

➤ Copperheads are venomous. This means that they are poisonous.

➤ The fangs of the copperhead are folded back in its mouth.

➤ A copperhead has a triangle-shaped head.

Length: 24 to 36 inches (61 to 91 cm)

Color: copper-colored with darker bands

Food: small rodents, lizards, frogs, and bugs

Where found: United States

Cottonmouth
(also called a water moccasin)
(Agkistrodon piscivorus)

➤ A cottonmouth swims with its whole body on top of the water.

➤ The cottonmouth hunts at night on land and in the water.

➤ The inside of its mouth looks like cotton.

Length: 30 to 48 inches (76 to 122 cm)

Color: dark green, dark brown, or black

Food: fish, other snakes, lizards, turtles, small birds, frogs, small alligators, and mice

Where found: near water in the southern United States

Rattlesnakes

(Crotalus)

- A rattlesnake's rattle makes a hissing sound.

- When a rattlesnake gets scared, it shakes its tail.

- A rattlesnake's rattle is made of the same stuff as your fingernails.

Length: 1 foot to 8 feet (0.3 to 2.4 m)

Color: many different patterns and shades of brown

Food: mice, rats, lizards, frogs, and rabbits

Where found: North, Central, and South America

Cobras

(Naja)

- Some cobras can spit their venom.
- King cobras are the only snakes that build nests for their babies.
- The venom of a king cobra can kill a full-grown elephant.

Length: 4 to 18 feet (1.2 to 5.5 m)

Color: many different colors

Food: birds, fish, frogs, toads, lizards, eggs, rabbits, rats, and other snakes

Where found: the Philippines, Asia, and Africa

Coral Snake

(Leptomicrurus micrurus)

➤ Coral snakes have small fangs.

➤ Coral snakes spend a lot of time underground, under rocks and fallen trees.

➤ The coral snake is venomous.

Length: 24 inches (61 cm)

Color: bands of black, yellow, and red

Food: other snakes, lizards, rats, and mice

Where found: all over the world

Black Mamba

(Dendroaspis polylepsis)

- The black mamba is the largest venomous snake in Africa.

- When a mamba gets scared, it can raise its body and head 4 feet (1.2 m) off the ground.

- A black mamba can strike from 4 to 6 feet (1.2 to 1.8 m) away.

Length: 14 feet (4.5 m)

Color: gray, but the inside of its mouth is black

Food: birds, mice, frogs, squirrels, and lizards

Where found: Africa

Another African snake, the green mamba, lives in trees.

Gaboon Viper

(Bitis gabonica)

➤ The fangs of this snake can be up to 2¼ inches (5.5 cm) long.

➤ Gaboon vipers make hissing noises to scare away animals that will eat them.

➤ Gaboon vipers move very slowly.

Length: 4 to 5 feet (1.2 to 1.5 m)

Color: patterns of brown, and tan stripes and triangles

Food: rats, mice, and monkeys

Where found: East and Central Africa

19

Sea Snakes

- There are about 70 different kinds of sea snakes.

- Sea snakes belong to the same family as cobras. They are not vipers.

- The sea snake breathes air just like other snakes, but it can stay underwater for a couple of hours.

- Sea snakes have a flat tail that looks like an oar. The tail helps them swim.

Length: 20 inches to 6 feet (50 cm to 2 m)

Color: many different colors

Food: fish, fish eggs, and eels; sea kraits only eat eel.

Where found: in shallow waters off the coast of Australia, and in the Indian and Pacific Oceans

Sea snakes have deadly venom, but the inland taipan from Australia is the most venomous snake in the world.

Lizards— Check It Out!

➤ Most lizards have four legs. Some lizards, like the glass snake, don't have any legs.

➤ All lizards have ear openings.

➤ Most lizards are fast runners. Some lizards climb trees. Others can move quickly across water.

➤ Lizards have small heads, short necks, and long bodies and tails.

Numbers: more than 4,000 different kinds

Where found: all over the world, except at the North and South Poles

Length: ½ inch to 10 feet (1.6 cm to 3 m)

Fun Facts

The smallest lizard, the dwarf gecko, can sit on the tip of your finger.

The six-lined racerunner is the fastest lizard. It can run 18 mph (29 kph).

Horned lizards can squirt blood from their eyes to scare away another animal or human.

The Komodo dragon is the world's largest lizard.

A basilisk can walk on water for about 15 feet (4.5 m). Then, it sinks and has to swim.

omodo Dragon

Monitor Lizard

- There are about 30 different kinds of monitor lizards.

- In Australia, monitor lizards are called goannas (say it like this: go-awn-az).

- When monitors get mad, they lash out with their tail.

- Monitors do not have fangs, but they have venom.

Length: 8 inches to 13 feet (20 cm to 4 m)

Color: many different colors

Food: carrion, giant land snails, insects, crocodiles, birds, eggs, crabs, fish, other lizards, snakes, birds, shrews, and squirrels

Where found: Africa, Asia, and Australia

Crocodile monitors have teeth like a T-rex.

Crocodile Monitor

Alligators and Crocodiles

- Alligators and crocodiles have a lot of teeth, but no fangs.
- Males grow larger than females.
- Alligators and crocodiles live at least 50 to 60 years in the wild.
- A throat pouch stops water from going down an alligator or crocodile's throat. This lets them eat underwater.

A crocodile skull fossil was discovered in Central Africa. The Sarchosuchus (SARK-oh-SOOK-us) lived during the time of the dinosaurs. This animal could have been 49 feet (15 m) long and weighed 17,500 pounds (6,619 kg)!

Differences Between Alligators and Crocodiles

Alligators are dark-colored with a round, broad nose. Crocodiles are grayish-green in color and have narrow noses that look like a triangle.

Alligators usually live in freshwater. Crocodiles usually live along the coast or saltwater areas.

Nile Crocodile

Numbers: 23 different kinds

Where found: the tropics in freshwater or saltwater

American Alligator

Saltwater Crocodile

(Crocodylus porosus)

- Saltwater crocodiles grab their prey and roll over. This is called a "death roll."
- These crocodiles are the largest living reptiles.
- Saltwater crocodiles will eat sharks.

Length: 23 feet (7 m)

Color: dark green and tan or light gray

Food: anything that gets close to the water, including fish, monkeys, wild pigs, and water buffalo

Where found: Southeastern Asia, Indonesia, the Philippines, and Australia

American Alligator

(Alligator mississippiensis)

- An American alligator's eyes are on top of its head.

- A male American alligator makes a loud roar that sounds like thunder.

- The female builds a nest made of mud, dead leaves, pine needles, and grasses.

Length: 15 feet (4.5 m)

Color: dark green or black

Food: insects, fish, frogs, birds, deer, raccoons, turtles, and other alligators

Where found: near freshwater in the southeastern United States

Mammals are warm-blooded animals.

This means that their body temperature always stays about the same. There are 4,000 kinds of mammals, including humans.

Mammals are found all over the world. Some mammals, like polar bears, live where it's cold. Others, like cheetahs, live where it's hot. Males usually are bigger than females.

Numbers: 4,000 different kinds
Where found: all over the world

Gorilla

Coyote

Common Vampire Bat

MAMMALS

Walrus

Tiger

- All mammals have hair or fur on their bodies.
- Most mammals are born live. They don't hatch from eggs.
- All baby mammals drink milk that comes from their mothers.
- Almost all mammals have teeth or fangs.

Hippopotamus

Giant Panda
(Ailuropoda melanoleuca)

- Pandas have very good eyesight.
- Pandas spend 10 to 16 hours a day eating.
- Pandas have thumbs. They use their thumbs to hold bamboo stalks.

Length: 4 to 6 feet (1.2 to 1.8 m)
Weight: 165 to 350 pounds (75 to 159 kg)
Color: black and white
Food: bamboo
Where found: forests in China

Grizzly Bear

(Ursus arctos)

- Grizzlies are a type of brown bear. They have a large hump of muscle on their shoulders.

- Grizzlies have long claws and sharp teeth.

- Grizzlies can run up to 35 mph (56 kph).

Length: 3 to 10 feet (1 to 3 m)

Weight: 250 to 600 pounds (113 to 272 kg)

Color: light cream, brown, or black fur

Food: plants, berries, large insects, and small mammals

Where found: North America

Polar Bear
(Ursus maritimus)

➤ Polar bears live in a cold part of the world called the Arctic. This is near the North Pole.

➤ Polar bears have a thick layer of fat called "blubber" under their skin. Blubber helps to keep them warm.

➤ Polar bears love to swim. Their fur is thick and waterproof.

Length: 7 to 9 feet (2.1 to 2.7 m)

Weight: 660 to 1,540 pounds (299 to 699 kg)

Color: white or cream fur; black skin

Food: seals, walruses, sea birds, lemmings, fish, and small water mammals

Where found: the Arctic

Red Fox

(Vulpes vulpes)

➤ Red foxes have an excellent sense of smell.

➤ Baby foxes are called "kits."

➤ Red foxes can hear very well. They can hear small animals digging underground.

Length: 3 to 5 feet (1 to 1.5 m) including tail

Weight: 4 to 15 pounds (2 to 7 kg)

Color: red, orange, or gray fur; black ears, limbs, and tail; white tip on the tail

Food: small mammals, insects, fruit, berries, and garbage

Where found: Canada, United States, Europe, Asia, and northern Africa

Coyote
(Canis latrans)

- Coyotes can run almost 40 mph (64 kph).

- Coyotes live for 10 to 15 years in the wild.

- Coyotes can jump an 8-foot (2.4-m) fence!

Length: 4 to 5½ feet (1.2 to 1.7 m) including tail

Weight: 33 to 44 pounds (15 to 20 kg)

Color: grayish-brown or yellowish-gray fur; black tip on the tail

Food: small mammals, reptiles, birds, fruit, vegetables, and carrion

Where found: North and Central America

Domestic Dogs
(Canis lupus familiaris)

- Dogs have sharp canine teeth (fangs).

- Domestic dogs live with humans. Many people have dogs as pets.

- Dogs are smart. They can be trained to do lots of things.

- Some dogs work with police officers. Others help blind people or act as guard dogs.

Numbers: hundreds of breeds

Height: 5 to 30 inches (13 to 76 cm)

Colors: many different colors

Food: store-bought dog food, small animals, and fruit

Where found: all over the world

African Lion
(Panthera leo)

- Lions live in groups called "prides."
- Lions work together to kill other animals for food.
- Male lions have lots of hair around their head and neck. This hair is called a "mane."

Length: 6.5 to 9 feet (2 to 2.7 m) including tail

Weight: 330 to 550 pounds (150 to 250 kg)

Color: golden to dark-brown fur; manes are golden or light brown

Food: wildebeest, zebra, impala, small rodents, and reptiles

Where found: grassy plains in Africa

Tiger
(Panthera tigris)

➤ Tigers can eat up to 90 pounds (41 kg) of meat in one day.

➤ Tigers are good swimmers.

➤ Tigers have striped fur. Their skin is striped, too! The stripes help them hide in the forest.

Length: 7 ½ to 13 feet (2.3 to 4 m)

Weight: 265 to 770 pounds (120 to 350 kg)

Color: orange fur with white and brown or black stripes

Food: deer, wild pigs, water buffalo, leopards, crocodiles, and small mammals

Where found: forests and swamps in Asia

Leopard
(Panthera pardus)

➤ Leopards are fast and very strong. They can jump more than 10 feet (3 m) in the air!

➤ Leopards live for 10 or 11 years in the wild.

➤ Leopards like to climb trees.

Length: 6 to 9½ feet (1.8 to 2.9 m) including tail

Weight: 100 to 200 pounds (45 to 91 kg)

Color: light-yellow to dark-brown with black rosettes (circles)

Food: antelope, gazelles, monkeys, snakes, warthogs, jackals, baboons, and carrion

Where found: Africa, the Middle East, and Asia

Snow leopards live in cold parts of Asia. They wrap their 3-foot- (1-m) long tail around them to keep warm.

51

Cheetah
(Acinonyx jubatus)

➤ Cheetahs are the fastest land animals. They can run up to 70 mph (113 kph)!

➤ The word "cheetah" means "spotted one."

➤ Cheetahs can't retract (bring in) their claws like other cats. This helps cheetahs grip the ground better when they run.

Length: 7 to 7½ feet (2.1 to 2.3 m) including tail

Weight: 85 to 145 pounds (39 to 66 kg)

Color: golden or tan fur with solid black spots; white fur on the throat and stomach

Food: antelope, gazelles, warthogs, impalas, rabbits, and birds

Where found: Africa and Asia

Another kind of big cat is the jaguar. Jaguars are good swimmers!

53

Domestic Cat
(Felis catus)

- Cats have sharp fangs.
- Domestic cats live alongside humans. Many people have cats as pets.
- Cats sleep a lot. They can spend up to 20 hours a day sleeping!
- Cats have excellent night vision.
- Cats have good balance. They can twist their bodies in midair to land feet first.

Numbers: more than 40 breeds

Weight: 5½ to 16 pounds (2.5 to 7 kg)

Color: many different colors

Food: store-bought cat food and small animals like mice, squirrels, rabbits, and birds

Where found: all over the world

55

Common Vampire Bat
(*Desmodus rotundus*)

➤ Vampire bats usually fly about 3 feet (1 m) above the ground.

➤ Vampire bats have special teeth that they use to make cuts in their prey. Then they lap up the blood.

➤ Each night, vampire bats drink about half their body weight in blood.

Length: body is 2 inches (5 cm); wingspan is 8 inches (20 cm)

Weight: 1.4 ounces (40 g)

Color: amber fur on the back; light-brown fur on the belly

Food: blood from cows, pigs, horses, and birds

Where found: Mexico, Central America, and South America

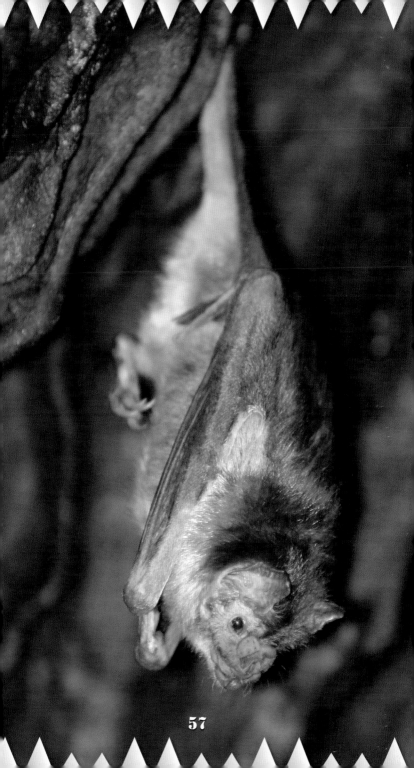

57

Hippopotamus

(Hippopotamus amphibious)

- Hippopotamuses live for about 40 years in the wild.

- A hippopotamus's teeth grow up to 28 inches (71 cm) long! Hippos use their teeth for fighting.

- Hippopotamuses are also known as river horses.

Length: 10 to 13 feet (3 to 4 m)

Weight: 3,300 to 7,000 pounds (1,500 to 3,200 kg)

Color: slate brown or muddy brown skin with purplish hues

Food: plants

Where found: near water in Africa

African Elephant
(Loxodonta Africana)

- Elephants are excellent swimmers.

- Elephants have tusks. Their tusks are large, pointed teeth.

- Elephants use their tusks to dig up food and lift objects.

Length: 23 to 29 feet (7 to 9 m) including tail

Weight: 8,000 to 13,000 pounds (3,600 to 5,900 kg)

Color: gray skin; white or cream-colored tusks

Food: bark, fruit, grass, and leaves

Where found: forests and savannas in Africa

There are two types of elephants: African and Asian. African elephants are larger.

61

Gorilla
(Gorilla gorilla)

➤ Gorillas live together in a group called a "troop."

➤ Gorillas live for about 35 years in the wild.

➤ Gorillas walk on their feet and knuckles.

Height: 4½ to 6 feet (1.4 to 1.8 m) at the shoulders

Weight: 150 to 500 pounds (68 to 227 kg)

Color: black skin covered with dark hair

Food: leaves, stems, fruit, seeds, and insects

Where found: along the equator in Africa

Atlantic Walrus

(Odobenus rosmarus rosmarus)

- Walruses have excellent hearing.

- Walruses have large tusks. Males use their tusks to show other walruses how strong they are. The tusks are also used for fighting.

- Walruses usually live in water that is around 330 feet (101 m) deep.

Length: 10 feet (3 m)

Weight: around 1,650 pounds (733 kg)

Color: cinnamon-brown skin

Food: clams, sea cucumbers, and other soft-bodied animals

Where found: in Arctic waters near Canada and Greenland

There are two kinds of walruses: Atlantic and Pacific. Pacific walruses are bigger.

Insects

exoskeleton

wings

head

antenn

6 legs

thorax

abdomen

Insects
1,000,000 kinds
Three body parts: head, thorax, abdomen
Most have six legs
Two antennae
Exoskeleton (skeleton outside body)
Most have wings and fly

Leafcutter Ants

Trapdoor Spider

BUGS

Praying Mantis

Honeybee

Arachnids

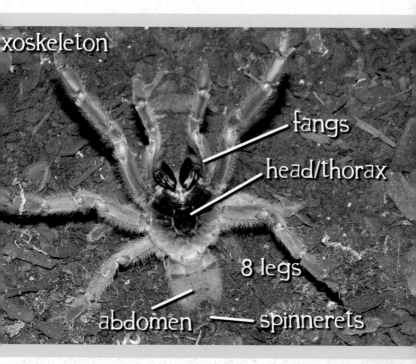

xoskeleton

fangs

head/thorax

8 legs

abdomen — spinnerets

Arachnids		
65,000 to 73,000 kinds		
Two body parts: head/thorax, abdomen Eight legs		
No antennae		
Exoskeleton		
Have no wings and do not fly		

Spiders—
Check It Out!

Spiders are arachnids. Some spiders have fangs to inject venom. This venom is used to kill and make a soupy mix of a spider's prey. They have tiny mouths that act like a straw. They drink the prey like a milkshake.

- Spiders have sensitive hairs on their legs. Hairs help spiders smell and feel things around them.
- Different spiders have from two to eight eyes.
- All spiders lay eggs.
- All spiders produce silk, which is a thin, strong thread.

Numbers: 40,000 different kinds
Where found: all over the world

The fear of spiders is called arachnophobia. (Say it like this: uh-rack-nah-fO-bE-uh.)

Black Widow

Wolf Spider

Tarantulas
(also called a bird spider, monkey spider, baboon spider, or rain spider)

➤ Tarantulas can be found in trees or on the ground.

➤ Some tarantulas make great pets.

➤ Tarantulas have eight eyes but cannot see very well.

Numbers: 800 different kinds

Length: 3 to 13 inches
(8 to 33 cm)

Color: many different colors; some have patterns

Food: insects, small mice, small fish, and reptiles

Where found: South America, Central America, United States, Asia, Europe, Africa, and Australia

Brown Recluse

(Loxosceles recluse)

- Bites from the brown recluse can make you feel like you have the flu. Sometimes wounds take a long time to heal.

- You'll find the brown recluse hunting at night.

- The brown recluse has very small fangs.

Length: ¼ to ¾ inch (6.5 to 19 mm)

Color: golden brown, with a shiny, dark-brown fiddle shape on its back

Food: insects

Where found: United States

Black Widow

(Latrodectus)

- A black widow's venom is more poisonous than a rattlesnake's.
- The black widow likes dark, warm places.
- Black widows make tangled webs near the ground.

Numbers: six different kinds

Length: ³⁄₄ to 1¹⁄₂ inches (2 to 3.8 cm)

Color: shiny black body; females have a red hourglass shape on the underside

Food: insects

Where found: warm parts of the world

Trapdoor Spider
(Ctenizidae)

➤ Trapdoor spiders dig a tunnel with a door that is made of soil, leaves, and spider silk.

➤ The trapdoor spider waits for prey by holding its door open with its feet. When its prey gets close, the spider closes the door quickly.

Numbers: 120 different kinds

Length: $\frac{1}{4}$ to $\frac{3}{4}$ inch (6.5 to 19 mm)

Color: brown with spotty markings

Food: insects, frogs, small birds, small snakes, mice, and small fish

Where found: Japan, Africa, South America, and North America

Golden Orb-weavers
(also called a banana spider)
(Nephila)

- Golden orb-weavers wrap their prey in their silk.

- These spiders are called "golden" because they make yellow silk.

- Golden orb-weavers' webs are very complex. They are remade every day.

Numbers: 27 different kinds

Length: ½ to 1 inch (1.5 to 3 cm)

Color: many, including reddish-brown, brown, gray, silver, and plum

Food: flies, beetles, and other insects

Where found: warm parts of the world

79

Wolf Spiders

(Lycosidae)

- Some wolf spiders use their silk to line their tunnels.
- These spiders live on the ground.
- A wolf spider has two eyes that face forward.

Numbers: more than 2,000 different kinds

Length: $\frac{1}{5}$ inch to 3 inches (1 to 8 cm)

Color: dark brown

Food: insects and other spiders

Where found: all over the world

Scorpion

(Buthoidea, Chactoidea, Chaeriloidea, Luroidea, Pseudochactoidea, Scorpionoidea)

- Scorpions have a stinger instead of fangs.
- Scorpions hunt at night.
- Some scorpions can go a year without eating.

Numbers: 1,500 different kinds

Length: ½ to 8½ inches
(1.2 to 22 cm)

Color: yellow, tan, brown, red, or black

Food: insects, spiders, centipedes, small mice, and rats

Where found: warm parts of the world

Some scorpions glow under blacklight.

83

Insects—
Check It Out!

Almost all of the animals on Earth are insects. Insects are cold-blooded, like reptiles. Insects have at least one set of wings; some have two. Millions of insects can live in a single area.

- Insects eat more plants than all other animals.
- Insects come in different shapes and sizes.
- One out of four animals on Earth is a beetle.

Numbers: 500,000 different kinds

Where found: all over the world

Praying Mantis

Insects can live in most environments.

Mosquito

Honeybee

85

Centipede
(Chilopoda)

➤ Centipedes are the only insects that have fangs.

➤ Some centipedes glow in the dark.

➤ Even though their name means "100 legs," not all centipedes have that many legs. Some have fewer than that. Some have even more!

Numbers: 3,000 different kinds

Length: 1 inch (2.5 cm)

Color: pale yellow to dark brown

Food: insects, earthworms, spiders, slugs, and other small animals

Where found: warm parts of the world

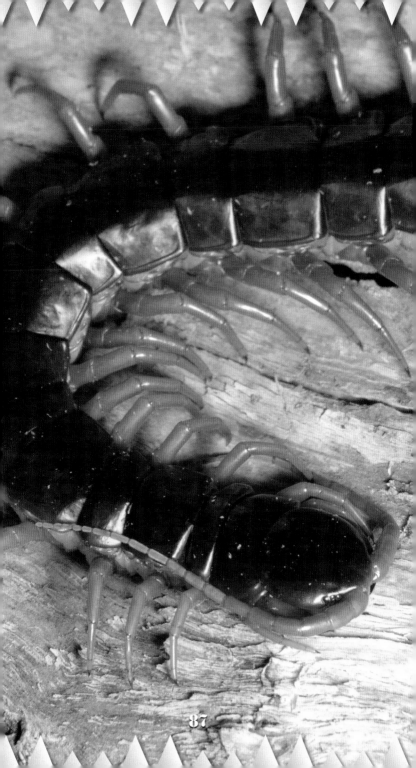

Praying Mantis
(Mantidae)

A praying mantis has strong mouth parts. It does not have fangs.

The praying mantis can turn its head around to face backward.

A praying mantis is a garden helper. It eats bugs that hurt vegetables that we eat.

Numbers: 2,300 different kinds

Length: 2 to 6 inches (5 to 15 cm)

Color: green

Food: insects, small birds, and lizards

Where found: In warm areas; some are found in the northern United States, Europe, and Siberia, where it is very cold

A praying mantis stalks its prey just like a cat.

Honeybee
(Apis mellifera)

- Bees have a stinger instead of fangs.
- Bees dance to show other bees where to find nectar.
- When a bee stings, it leaves the stinger and part of its body.

Numbers: many different kinds

Length: $2/5$ to $5/8$ inches (10 to 16 mm)

Color: golden brown and black

Food: flower nectar

Where found: all over the world

Africanized honeybees, or killer bees, came from Brazil. They are now spreading north.

91

Army Ant

(Eciton burchelli)

- Army ants hunt in swarms. They have strong mouth parts, but no fangs.
- Army ants move from place to place.
- Army ants work together to catch and carry off their prey.

Numbers: 100,000 to 2,000,000 ants per colony

Length: 1/10 to 1/2 inch (3 to 12 mm)

Color: golden to deep brown

Food: wasps, ant eggs, crickets cockroaches, tarantulas, scorpions, beetles, grasshoppers, and sometimes birds, snakes, and lizards

Where found: warm areas of Central and South America

Mosquito
(Culicidae)

- Mosquitoes have a mouthpart that acts like a straw. They do not have fangs.

- The mosquito is responsible for the most human deaths each year.

- Mosquitoes can detect their prey from 18 feet (5.5 m) away.

Numbers: about 2,700 different kinds

Length: ½ inch (15 mm)

Color: different shades of brown

Food: blood of other animals, including humans

Where found: warm parts of the world

Leafcutter Ant

(Atta cephalotes)

- Leafcutter ants have powerful jaws. They do not have fangs.
- The jaws vibrate very fast to slice off pieces of leaves.
- These ants can carry 20 times their own weight.

Numbers: 3 to 8 million ants per colony

Length: 1 inch (2.5 mm)

Color: green, red, brown, yellow, blue, or purple

Food: fungus (composted leaves and flowers)

Where found: Central and South America